This journal holds the peace, love, and writings of:

What does "harmony" mean to you? How can you have more harmony in your life?

Think about two of your favorite bands. How are they similar? How are they different?

Since I Started Kindergarten I am less shy and I have more friends. I also know math now.

Write a short story starting with this sentence:
It's always been easy for me to make friends.

Giraffes live in the African savanna. They are known for their long necks. Giraffes only eat plants. They are herbivores.

In what ways are you a good friend? What could you do better?

Decorate each heart with a unique doodle pattern.

Write a letter to your favorite band or singer, convincing them to play a concert at your school.

Ice cream vs. pudding: Which is yummier?
What's your favorite flavor?

Write about something that always makes you happy
to think about.

How did you feel the first time you heard your favorite song?

Your class gets to go on a field trip this year. Where should you go, and why?

Describe the best teacher you've ever had.

Write about something you wish you could do.

Violin vs. trumpet: Which one sounds better to you?
Which one would you like to learn to play?

Let your creativity flow as you color in this peace sign.

What's the one thing you would never, ever give up, and why?

What is your favorite type of music? Why?

Extroverts love to go out and socialize. Introverts like quiet time at home with a book or movie. Which one are you, and why?

Your favorite blog is giving away concert tickets to "the biggest fan" of your best friend's favorite band. Write them an email explaining why the tickets should go to your friend.

Write a short story starting with this sentence: Ethan looked at the clock again.

Write about your favorite celebrity with lots of descriptive words. Then read it to your friends and see if they know who you're talking about.

What is your all-time favorite food? Explain how to make it!
Why is it so yummy?

How is your morning routine different from your nighttime routine? Which one takes longer?

Write an argument to convince your parents about how they should get you a cat, dog, or other pet of your choice.

If you could have named yourself, what name would you have picked? Why?

Tell the story of a time when you found out you and someone else liked the same kind of music.

Think of a song that tells a story. How should the story go on after the song ends?

Look at the image on your favorite album, then look at one of your parents' albums. How are they different? How are they the same?

What was the last wish you made? Did it come true?

If it were New Year's Day, what would your resolution for the year be?

Write your own holiday song to the tune of one you like.

Decorate the peace sign with lots of colorful doodles!

You're throwing your friend a surprise party at your house. How do you convince them to come over at a specific time without giving away the real reason?

Describe the perfect winter day with friends.

Pick a theme song for each of the following, and explain why it represents them: your best friends; your favorite teacher; your pet or another animal you know well; and you.

Think about the hero and villain of one of your favorite movies. How are they alike?

You find out one of your friends has never heard of your favorite musician. Which playlists would you share with them, and why?

Describe your favorite genre of music to someone who has never heard it before.

Write a rhyming song to replace "Happy Birthday" on your best friend's next birthday.

Tell the story of the first time you met one of
your best friends.

Decorate the guitar with a fabulous doodle design fit for a rock star!
(Don't forget to add guitar strings when you're all done.)

Make a list of your top five "happy" songs and another of your top five "calming" songs. Compare how they sound.

Write a short story starting with this sentence:
Emma had heard the same song at least a hundred
times over the past three days.

What instrument do you want to learn to play? Why?

Your friend invites you to stay after school for their new club's meeting. Write a few text messages persuading your parents to pick you up late so you can go.

Set a goal that you can reach in the next week.
What can you do to achieve it?

Set a goal that you can reach in the next year.
What can you do to achieve it?

Tell the story of how your parents or grandparents met.

How is your daily routine different on a Wednesday and a Sunday? How is it the same?

My ULTIMATE PLAYLIST!

THE BEST SONGS EVER AS PICKED BY Me!

1. _____
2. _____
3. _____
4. _____
5. _____
6. _____
7. _____
8. _____
9. _____
10. _____

11. _____
12. _____
13. _____
14. _____
15. _____
16. _____
17. _____
18. _____
19. _____
20. _____

Write a short story that takes place at a summer camp.

Write a short story starting with this sentence:
It was the day before the school musical, and Shelly was coming down with the flu.

Describe how your family celebrates your birthday or favorite holiday.

Describe a time at school when you and someone else got over a big argument.

Write a short story about yourself traveling back in time. Where would you go and who would you meet?

Think of two completely different kinds of music. What do you like best about each one?

Think of a song that you like to listen to when you're sad. How does it make you feel better?

What fun, creative project have you been wanting to do?
List the things you'll need to do it, and how you'll make it.

Decorate the dove with your own beautiful pattern.

Your best friend is worried about a recital she has coming up. What do you say to support her?

If you could be any character in a book, movie, or TV show, who would you be? Why?

Tell the story of the best apology you have ever heard.

Tell the story of the best compliment you have ever
received or given.

Write a short story that takes place in the school auditorium.

If you could pick the theme for the next school dance, what would it be, and why?

Describe the perfect summer day with friends.

Think of an object that you see every day—your toothbrush, for example. Don't look at it, but describe it in words. Then go look at it. How did you do?

What is one trait you truly admire in each of
your best friends?

Think of a school subject you'd like to do better in. What are a few ways to improve how you do?

Write a short story starting with this sentence:
Sophia had a secret talent.

About the Artist

Jess Volinski is a graduate of the School of Visual Arts in New York, NY, and the author/illustrator of more than a dozen coloring and activity books, including *Notebook Doodles® Super Cute*, *Notebook Doodles® Go Girl!*, and *Notebook Doodles® Sweets & Treats*. Besides creating books, she currently licenses her art for the publishing, fashion, and tableware industries. Originally from Connecticut, Jess now lives in southern New Jersey with her husband and two kids.

Notebook Doodles® Activity Books

ISBN 978-1-64178-072-8

Fox Chapel Publishing makes every effort to use environmentally friendly paper for printing.

© 2019 by Jess Volinski and Quiet Fox Designs, www.QuietFoxDesigns.com, an imprint of Fox Chapel Publishing Company, Inc., 903 Square Street, Mount Joy, PA 17552.

We are always looking for talented authors and artists. To submit an idea, please send a brief inquiry to acquisitions@foxchapelpublishing.com.

Printed in China
First printing